T0199024

Arepas

Sennyo Ookami

Balboa Press books may be ordered through booksellers or by contacting:

Balboa Press
A Division of Hay House
1663 Liberty Drive
Bloomington, IN 47403
www.balboapress.com
1 (877) 407-4847

ISBN: 978-1-9822-5204-5 (sc)
ISBN: 978-1-9822-5205-2 (e)

Library of Congress Control Number: 2020914053

Print information available on the last page.

Balboa Press rev. date: 08/27/2020

BALBOA.PRESS
A DIVISION OF HAY HOUSE

Acknowledgment

"This book is dedicated to my beautiful twins Rosita & Tessita, you showed me the magic of love and inspired me to write books so you can read them as you grow older."

"The *harina pan* falls into the bowl."

"Then comes *el agua*."

"Don't forget un *poquito de sal*! There was something beautiful about how the salt fell into the bowl, tiny crystal fragments dancing their way into the *masa*."

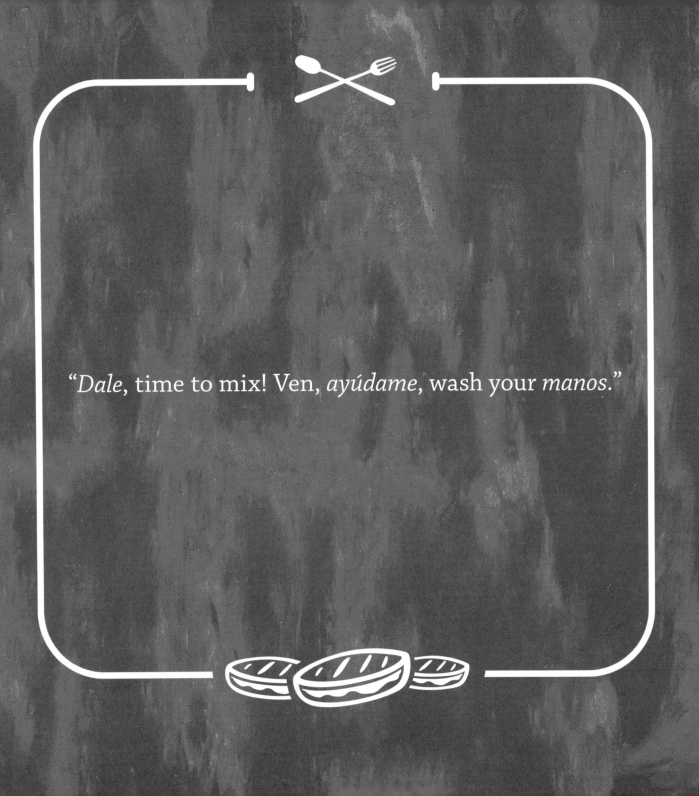

"*Dale*, time to mix! Ven, *ayúdame*, wash your *manos*."

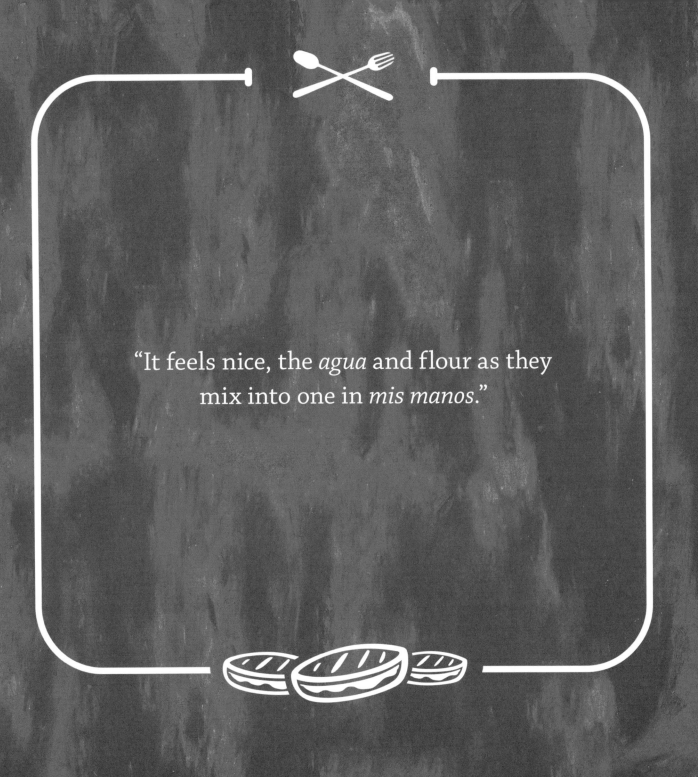

"It feels nice, the *agua* and flour as they mix into one in *mis manos*."

"We get one big fluffy *pelota*!"

"Shape Them..."

"Cook them…"

"Tap them, if they sound like a *tambor, están listas*!"

"Open it carefully with a knife, *cuidado*!
It's so *caliente*, *rellénalos*."

"Gracias and *buen provecho!"*

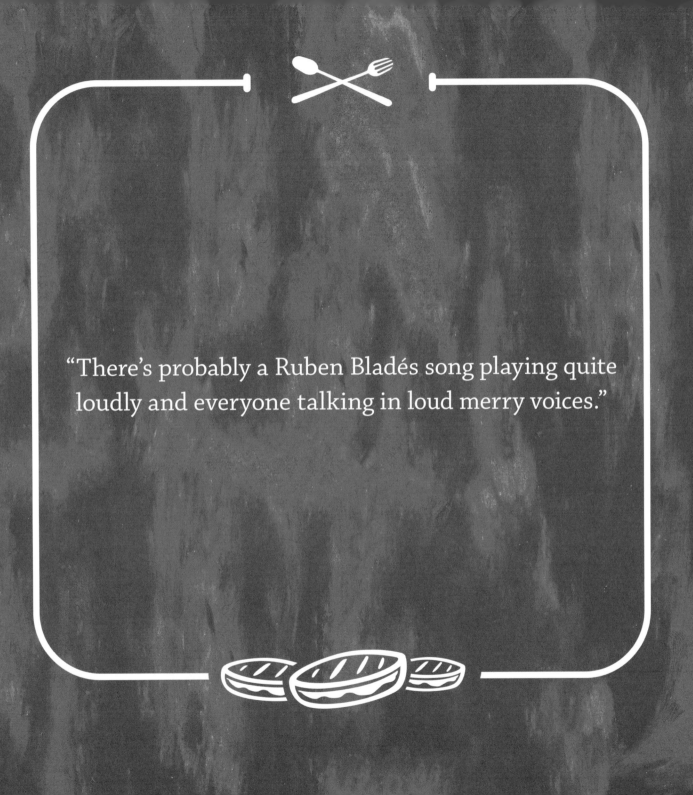

"There's probably a Ruben Bladés song playing quite loudly and everyone talking in loud merry voices."

Reference page:

- Arepa Mix: 1 cup of corn flour, 1 cup of water, 2 pinch of salt
- Cooking instructions: Cook on pan until golden on both sides, medium fire, then put in oven at 375 degrees fh for 10 min, tap them for sound.
- Spanish Word Glossary:

Harina pan	=	*Bread flour*
El agua	=	*Water*
Poquito de sal	=	*A little bit of salt*
Masa	=	*Dough*
Dale	=	*Go*
Ayúdame	=	*Help me*
Mis manos	=	*My hands*
Pelota	=	*Ball*
Tambor	=	*Drum*
Están listas	=	*They're ready*
Cuidado	=	*Careful*
Caliente	=	*Hot*
Rellénalos	=	*Stuff them*
Gracias	=	*Thank you*
Buen provecho	=	*Enjoy your meal*

Printed in the United States
By Bookmasters